W9-CLS-636

Secrets
of the
Congdon Mansion

Jaykay Publishing Inc.
Minneapolis, Minnesota 55415

© Copyright 1985 by Jaykay Publishing Inc.

All rights reserved. No portion of this book may be reproduced or transmitted in any form or by any means, electronic or mechanical, including photocopying, recording or by any information storage and retrieval system, without written permission of the publisher.

Jaykay Publishing Inc.
P.O. Box 15775
Minneapolis, Minn. 55415

ISBN 0-9613778-1-X
Printed in the U.S.A.
Revised 1994

The Contents

The Introduction

Don't expect to get all your questions answered when you take a tour of the Congdon Mansion.

To get the inside story, you need more information than the tour guides will give you. You need the information available here, in The Secrets of the Congdon Mansion.

The Official Tour, of course, is well worthwhile. You'll learn that the mansion is a striking example of early 20th Century Jacobian architecture. You'll be told about the design and decor of the building, and you'll see state-of-the-art woodwork from the early 1900s.

But for many people, those aren't the big attractions of the Congdon Mansion.

For them, the mansion is best known as the site of the Congdon Murders, the place where 83-year-old heiress Elisabeth Congdon was murdered June 27, 1977 — smothered in her bed with a pink satin pillow.

Congdon's night nurse also died that night — beaten to death with a candlestick holder as she tried to defend the helpless old woman.

The prosecutor called it a crime of greed. The murderer wanted a share of the inheritance from the dead woman's vast estate, he said.

It was a complex and intriguing murder case. At times, the plot seemed to leap from the pages of an Agatha Christie novel, and each succeeding chapter made front-page news throughout Minnesota. It catered, somehow, to the public's fascination with murder and mansions and money.

But you won't hear a word about the Congdon Murders on the Official Tour. The volunteer guides won't tell you which bedroom was Miss Congdon's, or where the murderer broke into the house, or how he escaped.

That's the reason for this book, to answer those questions and more; to tell you the Secrets of the Congdon Mansion.

The
Murders

In a cemetery next to the mansion he waited, huddled next to a tree, trying to stay out of sight. He was jumpy, drunk and desperate. Through the woods, he heard cars race by on London Road, busy even at this late hour. Behind him, waves from Lake Superior broke along the shore, steady, insistent, growing louder each minute.

Finally, after more than an hour, he steeled his nerve and clenched his teeth. It was time. He made his way along the back of the mansion, to a covered patio area — the place the family called the subway. The windows had been removed for the summer, so he stepped right in.

Using a rock, he broke a hole in the window of the billiard room. He reached inside, unlatched the window, and opened it wide. He climbed into the room, then paused a moment and listened. Nothing stirred.

Stepping gingerly, sometimes crunching the broken glass strewn on the floor, he felt his way around the large billiard table, and walked out into the hallway. Still no alarm.

Around to the right he found the stairs. Quietly, gently, he went up, step by step. He made it to the main floor. Just one more flight to go and he'd find the bedroom of Elisabeth Congdon, his wealthy mother-in-law.

The plan was simple. Miss Congdon was 83 and partially paralyzed. No one would be surprised if she died one night in her sleep. All he had to do was make sure tonight was the night, then slip quietly out the door and get back to Colorado. He and his wife then would receive an inheritance worth millions of dollars, more than enough to pay the thousands of dollars in debts that were piling up back home.

(Later, he denied that he planned to murder the old lady. He said he wanted to burglarize the mansion and sell the stolen items to pay the bills. Police investigators, though, maintain that murder was the motive.)

Nearly to the top of the stairs, he stumbled, breaking his trance. He took the pint of vodka from his pocket and took another drink. Then he shook his head to clear the tangled knot of liquor and fear. He started back up the stairs.

Suddenly, a door opened in the hallway above.

A ribbon of light swept past him. A woman with a flashlight came out the door, straight at him. He shouted. She screamed. They struggled for a moment, but she was old and much smaller; he overpowered her easily. Her body fell to the landing midway between floors. Shivering with fear, he raced up the stairs, more anxious than ever to finish the job and get out of there.

But below him, on the landing, the woman moaned. He had to stop that noise.

From a table at the top of the stairs, he grabbed a 12-inch brass candlestick holder, and walked down to the moaning woman. He beat her on the head and arms, fracturing her skull and breaking her jaw on both sides. Reaching out blindly, she clawed at the killer's head, and pulled out several locks of his hair. The hair remained clutched tightly in her hands as she died.

Bloodied from the encounter, the murderer rushed up the stairs and found Miss Congdon's bedroom — the first door from the stairs around to the right. The old woman was asleep. He pulled a pillow from beneath her head and held it firmly against her face. Miss Congdon awoke and struggled with her attacker. She fought vigorously, turning her head from side to side. Skin from her nose rubbed off on the pillow as she tried to escape. It took nearly four minutes, but then she, too, was dead.

The killer methodically opened all the drawers in the room. He found a small, wicker basket in the closet and filled it with jewelry. He took a sapphire and diamond ring off the dead woman's finger and a gold watch from her wrist and put them in the basket. As he was leaving, he saw a gold, Byzantine coin in a memorabilia box. He took that, too.

He ducked into a small bathroom across the hall and washed his bloody hands, wiping them on his shirt and pants, which were already streaked with blood. On a bed in an adjoining bedroom, he saw a purse and a set of keys. He grabbed the keys and ran down the stairs, past the dead woman lying stretched across the window seat on the landing.

He ran out the front door and matched the car keys with a 1976 white-and-tan Granada, parked in the driveway. Then he drove to the Minneapolis-St. Paul International Airport, stopping only once to ask directions.

The
Congdons

I t was a hot Sunday afternoon at the Congdon Mansion on the shores of Lake Superior in Duluth. Elisabeth Congdon and her attendants had just returned from a weekend at the summer place, on the Brule River in northwestern Wisconsin.

As Miss Congdon rested in her bedroom, one of the nurses unpacked the clothes from the trip, and put a small wicker basket away in the closet. Miss Congdon went to sleep shortly before 11 p.m., without her usual medication. "She was tired and very happy and went right to sleep," according to the nurse. It was June 26, 1977.

Those weekend trips away from the mansion weren't easy for Miss Congdon — Miss Elisabeth as she was affectionately called. She was 83-years-old and partially paralyzed by a stroke eight years earlier. But she tried to keep a normal routine. She had some assistance; around-the-clock nurses and the best medical care money could buy. She was, after all, one of the richest women in Minnesota: the last remaining child of Chester Congdon and heiress to his fortune.

Chester Congdon had been a legend in his own time, at least in northeast Minnesota. He built a fortune in the burgeoning iron mining business at the turn of the century, and then in 1905, he began building the mansion, Glensheen. It was the best money could buy; worth $864,000 in 1905 dollars. Complete with marble and oak, gold leaf and teak trim, and furnishings from around the world. The property included 7½ beautifully landscaped acres, with a creek running through the property to the lake.

Chester and his wife, Clara, had seven children. Young Elisabeth was 14 when the family moved into the mansion in 1908. Soon afterward, Elisabeth went East, to Vassar College. Then she returned to Duluth and was active in many charitable activities. She was the first president of Duluth's King's Daughters Society, which later became the Junior League of Duluth.

Elisabeth Congdon

Elisabeth never married, but she adopted two daughters in the 1930s, an unusual event at the time. The two girls grew up at the mansion, with all the comforts of the rich. One daughter was Jennifer, who eventually married Charles Johnson and lived a relatively uneventful life with him in Racine, Wisconsin.

The other daughter was Marjorie, whose life was, well, quite eventful.

Congdon Notes

Elisabeth Congdon allowed the Mansion to be used as the filming site of the 1972 Hollywood movie "You'll Like My Mother," starring Patty Duke. The film, occasionally seen on late night television, is about a young widow who visits her mother-in-law in a large family mansion. She doesn't realize, however, that her mother-in-law has been murdered, and that one of the murderers is impersonating the dead woman.

Shortly after the real Congdon murders, a downtown Duluth theater revived the film for a short time.

The
Daughter

Marjorie was living in Colorado during the summer of 1977; in Golden, a suburb of Denver and the home of Coors Beer.

Her husband, Roger Caldwell, was drinking heavily and the couple had serious financial troubles. Roger was Marjorie's second husband. Her first marriage, to Richard LeRoy of Minneapolis, ended in divorce in 1971. They had seven children.

Throughout her life, Marjorie had been known as a spendthrift. For example, she bought 300 to 350 riding habits for her two daughters when they needed only three apiece, according to one of the daughters.

Marjorie moved to Colorado in 1975 with her youngest son, Ricky, then 15. Her other children remained in Minnesota.

In Colorado, she met Caldwell, who was also divorced. They were married in March 1976, in Littleton, Colo. Roger later told his family that he didn't know about Marjorie's money right away. This is how he described their first financial chat:

She told him "I have some money."

He said: "Good, because I don't."

"No, really, Roger. I do."

"What's some money?" he asked. Then she told him and he almost fell over.

Marjorie did, indeed, have some money — at least in theory. Upon the death of her mother, Marjorie stood to inherit a goodly share of the Congdon estate. In addition, Miss Congdon had set up two trusts for Marjorie and her family in 1968. At one time, the trusts were worth well over $1 million. But Marjorie drew substantial sums from the trusts, as much as $105,000 in one year. Apparently she didn't always pay attention to the limits of her bank account. In 1975, the bank handling the trusts asked a judge for permission to stop paying her bills, if the bank felt the payments were not in her best interests or those of her family.

Marjorie Caldwell

In 1976, a Minneapolis judge wrote that: "It is all too apparent from the evidence that Mrs. LeRoy (Marjorie) . . . tended to spend sums of money greatly in excess of the income available to her from the two trusts."

Congdon Notes

Marjorie Caldwell's first husband, Richard LeRoy, is a former chairman of the Minnesota T (Taxpayers) Party. He was Minneapolis chairman of Minnesotans for Goldwater in 1964 and was a Minneapolis Library Board member. He ran unsuccessfully for the Minneapolis School Board in 1967. The couple had seven children. They were divorced in 1971 .

The
Son-in-law

After her marriage to Roger Caldwell, Marjorie kept up a torrid spending pace. In late 1976 and early 1977, she signed contracts for more than $750,000 worth of Colorado ranch land. But all the deals eventually fell through, when she failed to come up with the money.

The couple had three Jeeps repossessed by a Colorado bank in June 1977, and a horse trainer said Roger Caldwell bought a $6,000 horse from him with a check that bounced.

The Caldwells were apparently in desperate financial straits when, on May 25, 1977, Roger Caldwell flew to Duluth, alone, for his first visit with his mother-in-law, Elisabeth Congdon.

During the visit, Roger Caldwell spent half an hour at the Congdon Mansion, chatting with Miss Congdon. They talked in the library, on the main floor of the house, just inside the front door. That is the only part of the house Caldwell saw that day.

Roger did not discuss money with Miss Congdon. All her financial matters were handled by trustees of the estate. Caldwell made a point to meet with them.

He told them he needed money, $800,000, so he and Marjorie could buy a ranch. He even produced a letter from a prominent physician, saying Marjorie's son, Ricky, needed to live in the mountains because of an asthma condition. The letter, it turned out later, was forged.

The trustees turned down Roger's request for money.

A week later, Roger met with another Congdon family member in Denver, and again asked for money. Caldwell told the man that he and

Roger Caldwell

Marjorie were desperately short, and even had used slugs in a pop machine. They needed $81,000 right away, Roger said, to pay off debts that could land them in jail.

But once again, Roger returned to Golden without any money.

Congdon Notes

Roger Caldwell was raised in Latrobe, Pa., a small town near Pittsburgh. Latrobe is best known as the hometown of Arnold Palmer and Fred (Mr.) Rogers. Caldwell ran track and played football in high school. His father was a steel worker for 40 years. Two of Caldwell's three brothers still live in Latrobe. One is a city policeman. Caldwell married his childhood sweetheart in 1954, but they were divorced 20 years later in Littletown, Colo.

The Scene
of the Crime

At 7 a.m., on the dot, the morning nurse reported for duty at the Congdon Mansion. It was Monday, June 27, 1977.

She was relieving Velma Pietila, who'd been working all night at the mansion, caring for Miss Elisabeth. Velma had retired as a Congdon nurse in May, but had agreed to fill in for the night, because the regular nurse was on vacation and the relief nurse had company.

When the morning nurse went up to Miss Congdon's room that morning, she saw Velma's body on the landing. "Oh no," she thought, "Velma's had a stroke and fell down the stairs." She checked for a pulse. There was none. Then she realized that Miss Congdon was upstairs, alone. She ran up to the room and saw the pillow over the old woman's face. She called the police.

Publicly, police said it was a robbery. "An empty jewelry box was on the floor of the bedroom and the room was ransacked," said Police Inspector Ernie Grams.

But behind the scenes, police already were tracking two suspects in the case: Marjorie and Roger Caldwell. Congdon family members had told police immediately that they suspected the Caldwells, primarily because of the couple's financial troubles.

Within hours after the murders were discovered, a Congdon relative in Denver hired a private investigator, to protect his family from the Caldwells.

Using the tips from the family, Duluth police began an intense investigation. They checked out the Holland House Motel in Golden, Colorado, where the Caldwells were living. They checked the Radisson Hotel in Duluth, where the Caldwells stayed during Miss Congdon's funeral. And they checked the Holiday Inn Airport South in Bloomington, where the Caldwells spent several nights after the funeral.

Ernie Grams

At each place, police found evidence. Enough, they believed, to link Roger Caldwell to the murders.

In the early morning hours of July 6, Roger Caldwell was arrested in a suburban Minneapolis hospital room. He had collapsed in the Bloomington motel the day before, and was recovering when police arrived.

Congdon Notes

Duluth Chief of Detective Ernie Grams was called the "Duluth Sleuth" by the media during the murder investigation, as he chomped on his ever-present cigar during long days on the case. Other agencies that worked with him were: the State Patrol, Golden, Colo. police, Twin Cities airport police, police officers from the Minneapolis suburbs of Fridley, Bloomington and St. Louis Park and the Hennepin County Sheriff's deputies.

Grams was later elected St. Louis County Sheriff.

On Sept. 22, 1986, Grams died when his car left the road and hit a tree. In a special election that year, Police Lt. Gary Waller — the chief investigator on the Congdon case — was elected sheriff.

The State
vs.
Roger Caldwell

A judge ruled that too much publicity in the case meant Caldwell would not receive a fair trial in Duluth, so the trial was moved to Brainerd, a quiet resort town in north central Minnesota.

Jury selection began in April 1978. The attorneys spent nearly a month questioning 81 potential jurors before seven women and five men were selected.

Then Prosecutor John DeSanto began to methodically present the case of The State of Minnesota vs. Roger Sipe Caldwell.

There was no direct evidence to link Caldwell to the crimes, DeSanto admitted. No eyewitnesses or fingerprints on the candlestick holder. But DeSanto presented 100 witnesses whose testimony wove a web of circumstantial evidence, which, DeSanto said, proved that Caldwell was guilty, beyond a reasonable doubt.

The motive was greed, he said. The Caldwells were deep in debt and needed the inheritance to pay their bills and buy a ranch in Colorado. Witnesses in the trial outlined the Caldwell's financial troubles: the repossessed Jeeps, the trip to Duluth to ask for money, the ranch purchases that fell through. "This was a very extravagant, spendthrift, dream-world type lifestyle for this unemployed fortune seeker," DeSanto told the jury. "And this financial pressure continued to build until that fatal day."

DeSanto told the jury about a will, prepared by Marjorie Caldwell just three days before the murders. The will, found by police in the Caldwells' safe deposit box, gave Roger control of more than $2.5 million of his wife's expected inheritance. DeSanto called the will "the carrot," intended to entice Caldwell to commit the murders.

● Police testified that they found jewelry and a wicker basket in the Caldwells' Bloomington motel room. It was the same jewelry and basket

John DeSanto

taken from Elisabeth Congdon's bedroom, a Congdon employee told the jury.

● Then there was the gold coin, an old Byzantine coin taken from Miss Congdon's room the night of the murders. Police found the coin a few days later in the Caldwell's Colorado mail box. It had been mailed from Duluth on June 27, the day of the murders, and was addressed to Roger Caldwell in his own handwriting. A thumbprint on the envelope was Roger Caldwell's, according to the testimony of a fingerprint expert. DeSanto told the jury that Caldwell had mailed the coin to Colorado, possibly as a signal that the murders had been committed.

● Police also had other circumstantial evidence. In the Caldwells' Duluth hotel room police found a receipt for $56 from the Twin Cities Airport gift shop. They believed the receipt, dated June 27, was for a suede suit bag. Police found such a bag in the Caldwells' Bloomington motel room.

● The prosecution had some unexpected help in the case, when two employees of the airport gift shop pointed to Roger Caldwell in the courtroom and said he was the man who bought the suede suit bag on the morning after the murders. Earlier in the trial, DeSanto had told the jurors that the two employees would not be able to identify Caldwell. But sitting on the witness stand, each one pointed to Caldwell and said he was the man she'd seen in the gift shop, nearly one year earlier. Caldwell's lawyer, Doug Thomson, tried to discredit the identifications by stressing to the jury that the employees had failed to identify pictures of Caldwell when questioned by police four days after the murders.

There were several holes in the state's case. The major one was proving how Caldwell got back to Colorado from the Minneapolis airport. It appeared there were only two commercial flights he could have taken that day. Police checked the airline records for both flights, but could not find Caldwell's name or a likely alias.

Marjorie's son, Ricky, also testified that he had seen Roger Caldwell in bed in Colorado on the night of the murders. He said he looked into the bedroom used by his mother and Caldwell, and saw "two lumps under the covers." He said he did not see Caldwell's face.

During the trial, some observers raised questions about the case against Caldwell. If he killed the women, why did he bring the stolen jewelry back to Colorado, and then bring it to the Twin Cities? Why did he mail the gold coin to himself? None of his fingerprints were found in the mansion. Why was he so careful there, but so careless with the jewelry and gold coin? Why did he rely on Velma Pietila's car for the get-away? Pietila was filling in that night for a vacationing nurse. How did he know her car, or any car, would be available?

Defense attorney Doug Thomson pointed to these inconsistencies in the case, and suggested Caldwell had been framed.

But DeSanto told the jury that Caldwell made "stupid moves" because he "wasn't himself after the murders, or maybe he was feeling a false sense of security because he thought he had gotten away with it."

One other apparent hole in the prosecution's case was cleared up before the trial ended. Police had found two fingerprints at the mansion which didn't match up with anyone involved in the case. They definitely weren't Caldwell's, and Thomson hinted that they might belong to the "real killer."

Police checked further, though, and cleared up the mystery. One of the fingerprints belonged to a part-time nurse at the mansion.

Doug Thomson

The other print, found on the bathroom sink where the killer washed up, belonged to Duluth Police Sgt. Gary Waller, the chief investigator in the case.

Testimony in the trial took two months. The jurors began deliberations on July 6, 1978. They spent three days in a small room in the Brainerd County Courthouse, arguing back and forth about the case.

At 4:30 p.m. on the third day, they reached a consensus. The courtroom was silent as the jurors marched to their places. The court clerk took the verdict sheet and read the word: "Guilty." Roger Caldwell looked at the jurors and softly said, "You're wrong."

The judge then asked each of the jurors if they agreed with the verdict. All 12 said yes. One woman cried as she replied.

Later, several jurors said the sentiment in the jury room initially seemed to be for acquittal. But by the time the first vote was taken, it was 7 to 5 for guilty. The discussions continued until everyone agreed with the judgment of guilt.

Two days later, Roger Caldwell was sentenced to two consecutive life terms in Stillwater Prison. St. Louis County District Court Judge Jack Litman called the murders "brutal, heinous, awful and awesome."

The next day, Marjorie Caldwell was charged with conspiring with her husband to kill her mother and the nurse. She was released on $100,000 bond, after turning herself in to Duluth police.

Part Two of the Congdon Murder Trials had begun.

The State vs. Marjorie Caldwell

This time again, a judge ruled that excessive publicity made it impossible for a fair trial to be held in Duluth. Marjorie Caldwell's trial was moved to Hastings, a southern St. Paul suburb.

In the beginning, Marjorie's trial was similar to Roger's. Jury selection was lengthy, taking nearly three weeks. And again, John DeSanto was the prosecutor.

When testimony began, April 26, 1979, DeSanto again told of the Caldwell's extravagant life style and subsequent debts. He told the jury that Marjorie "dominated and manipulated Roger from the very beginning." She planned the murders; he committed them "with the assurance he would get a certain amount of the money," DeSanto said.

Much of DeSanto's evidence in this trial remained the same; the financial problems, the suit bag, the gold coin, the stolen jewelry. In addition. he outlined conflicting stories Marjorie had told about Roger's whereabouts on the night of the murders. She told her son that she and Roger would be looking at real estate all weekend; she told a real estate agent that Roger was in Colorado Springs; she told a lawyer that Roger had just gone to a convenience store and she told someone else that Roger was visiting a sick friend at a Denver hospital, DeSanto said.

The defense in this trial was much more aggressive. Ron Meshbesher, Marjorie's attorney, had used the intervening year well; he had some surprises for the prosecution. Meshbesher began by attacking the police investigation of the case. Under cross-examination by Meshbesher, a police officer admitted that he used the toilet and sink in the upstairs bathroom while investigating the murders. Other police officers said that photographs taken during the investigation were lost, and when duplicates were made, there was confusion about who took the photos and when they were taken.

Ronald Meshbesher

Marjorie's former lawyer, David Arnold, caused quite a stir when he testified that Marjorie "loved her mother and never spoke an unkind word about her." Arnold also said that Marjorie thought she might not inherit much of the Congdon estate because she was adopted.

An even bigger stir came during testimony by and about William Furman, a Colorado private investigator. Furman was hired for protection by Congdon family members in Denver only hours after the murders were discovered. Later Furman was told to investigate Marjorie and Roger. During that investigation, Furman and his associates supposedly followed the Caldwells from Golden to Duluth and then to Bloomington. In each place, incriminating evidence against the Caldwells was found. Meshbesher hinted to the jury that Furman might have planted that evidence, as part of an elaborate scheme to frame the Caldwells for the murders.

Duluth police were also aware of Furman's investigation, but soon discounted its value. They suspected that Furman never went to Duluth or Bloomington, but merely submitted a bill for the expenses in an attempt to defraud Thomas Congdon.

When Furman was called to the witness stand, he refused to answer 59 questions, claiming the Fifth Amendment right against self-incrimination. Furman remained a mystery man in the case.

Another surprise came late in the trial, when a Golden, Colorado waitress testified that she had seen Roger Caldwell only hours before the murders were committed. Candace Byers said she saw Caldwell coming down the stairs of the Holland House Motel at 10 p.m., Mountain Time, on the day before the murders. If that was true, it appeared unlikely that Caldwell could have made it to Duluth in time to kill the women later that night.

Byers' testimony came as quite a shock to the prosecution. She had not testified in Roger's trial. When questioned by police just days after the murders, Byers said she had last seen Caldwell two days before the women were killed, and said nothing about seeing him the night of the murders. At the trial, she explained her confusion to the jury: "I was real nervous talking to the police. I just wanted them to leave. I had customers waiting for me and they were staring at me."

It wasn't until three months before Marjorie's trial, when questioned by Meshbesher's investigators, that Byers told anyone about seeing Caldwell that night. Even then she didn't go to the police. The investigators "asked me not to pass it around," she said.

Perhaps the biggest blow to the prosecution's case, though, came when a fingerprint expert from Maryland, hired by DeSanto, testified that Roger Caldwell's thumbprint was not on the envelope containing the gold coin.

In Roger's trial, experts had matched the thumbprint to Roger Caldwell. It was a significant part of the evidence, because the postmark on the envelope placed Caldwell in Duluth on the day of the murders. Some of the jurors in that trial said the thumbprint helped them convict Roger.

But suddenly, the print didn't count anymore and the case against the Caldwells looked a bit shaky.

At the end of the trial, Meshbesher wove an elaborate frame-up theory to convince the jury of Marjorie's innocence. Furman and his friends had planted the evidence against the Caldwells, he said, so Marjorie would be denied her rightful inheritance. Even if Roger Caldwell had killed the women, his wife knew nothing about it, Meshbesher argued. Caldwell was a drunk and sometimes went on binges for days at a time, he said.

The jury deliberated for nine hours. Marjorie sobbed silently as jurors entered the courtroom; when the verdict "not guilty" was read, she cried openly. Meshbesher had tears in his eyes. So did John DeSanto's mother. DeSanto did not.

After the trial, the jurors appeared sympathetic to Marjorie. They invited her to a party later in the week. Marjorie told reporters she was tired and a little wobbly in the knees. Still, her troubles were not over.

The
Inheritance

When Marjorie walked out of the Hastings courtroom she was a free woman, but not a rich one. Her share of the Congdon inheritance, $8 million, was still tied up in the courts.

Four of Marjorie's children had filed suit in 1977 trying to prevent her from sharing in the inheritance. State law forbids anyone involved with a murder from inheriting money from the deceased.

This probate matter dragged on even after Marjorie's acquittal in the murder trial. The state supreme court ruled that a civil trial could be held to decide the inheritance issue, without subjecting Marjorie to double jeopardy.

The case was finally settled out of court on June 29, 1983. Under the agreement, Marjorie and her children will share the $8 million, although lawyers and creditors skimmed more than $2 million off the top.

Marjorie was to receive slightly more than one-fourth of a $6 million trust left under her grandfather's will. The remainder will go to the children. Marjorie, though, will receive the interest from one-third of the children's share as long as she lives. The children also shared a second trust, worth about $2 million. Attorney's fees and debts were deducted proportionally from the two trusts.

Family members believe she is getting about $40,000 per year from her trust.

When told of the arrangement in 1987, Roger Caldwell, then living on welfare in Pennsylvania, said this:

"No matter how much money she has, it will never be enough."

The Deal

After Marjorie's acquittal, Roger Caldwell immediately appealed his conviction. He claimed that new evidence from her trial — primarily the false thumbprint — would prove his innocence. The Minnesota Supreme Court agreed. On August 7, 1982, the justices ordered a new trial.

The thumbprint, you'll remember, was found on an envelope in the Caldwell's Colorado hotel. It had a Duluth postmark from the day of the murders and was a major factor in Roger's conviction. At Marjorie's trial, though, it was shown that the thumbprint was not Roger's, after all.

Prosecutor John DeSanto was shocked at the Supreme Court's ruling. "There's no question that we have the right man in jail," he said.

Caldwell was released from prison pending the new trial and returned home to Latrobe, Pa. On the day of his release, he was asked about his plans. "Maybe I'll become a tour guide at the Congdon Mansion," he said. One of his relatives later said: "Roger has a black sense of humor."

Officials in Duluth had vowed they'd go after Caldwell again in court, but as the time grew near, that resolve began to fade. Neither side really wanted another trial. Roger didn't want to risk another conviction and the prosecutors wanted to avoid the cost of another trial, especially when there was no guarantee that they'd win without the fingerprint evidence.

So they struck a deal. On July 5, 1983, in a closed Duluth courtroom, Caldwell pleaded guilty to two counts of second degree murder. In return, he was allowed to go free — having served just over five years in prison.

At first glance, it doesn't seem like much of a deal from the prosecution's side. Caldwell confessed to two brutal murders, then was allowed to get out of jail —free. It was a classic example of plea bargaining, with all its advantages and disadvantages.

Technically, the murders were now solved, without the risk and expense of another trial. Still, many wondered at the wisdom of the deal and the fairness of the legal system.

Back in Latrobe, Caldwell's family still refused to believe he'd been involved in the murders. "He had to plead guilty to get out of jail," one said. "He would have been crazy not to."

Roger himself said just a week after his release: "If I did it, I should still be in jail. If I didn't do it, why did they spend all those years going after me?"

Roger decided to stay in Latrobe after making the deal, even though the entire town knew about his troubles with the law. (Until Caldwell's release from prison, the local media had ignored his story. But then a St. Paul reporter tipped off the Latrobe newspaper about Roger and it became front page news.)

Roger was unable to find a job in Latrobe, and went on welfare.

Marjorie, meanwhile, refused to stay out of the public eye.

She married Wallace Hagen, an old family friend, in a 1981 North Dakota ceremony. Somehow, she neglected to divorce Roger first. Bigamy charges were filed in March, 1983, but North Dakota officials decided not to seek extradition. So it's unlikely she'll ever face prosecution.

When I learned about the Hagen wedding, I asked Roger about his divorce. He said there hadn't been one, and seemed surprised and hurt that Marjorie had remarried.

Trouble followed Marjorie back to Minnesota. Early in 1983, she was charged with arson and insurance fraud for burning down a suburban Mound home.

Meshbesher defended her again, but this time, a jury found her guilty. Hennepin County District Court Judge Robert Schiefelbein sentenced her to 2½ years in prison and a $10,000 fine.

The day before she was sentenced, Marjorie was arrested in St. Louis Park for shoplifting a $7.99 bottle of vitamins from the Byerly's store.

In January, 1985, all her appeals ran out, and she began serving her arson sentence at the Shakopee Women's Prison.

She was released on parole in October, 1986, and went to spend the winter in Arizona with Hagen. Family members said she then began a pattern of spending the winters in Arizona, and the summers in Minnesota.

The Aftermath

By his own account, Roger spent six miserable years in Latrobe following his release from prison. He was broke, and became increasingly bitter as he failed to adjust to life on the outside.

At first, he seemed confident he could overcome the stigma of the murder convictions. I visited him in 1983, just days after his plea bargain, and found him hopeful and energetic. He wanted to find work and put the prison days behind him. He hadn't heard from Marjorie for years, but suspected her lawyers might work out some sort of divorce deal — so he'd collect at least a little of the Congdon money, after all.

It never happened. Caldwell stayed on welfare, getting $186 per month. He shared a small apartment near the old railroad depot with a woman friend — for companionship and to save money. They survived with food stamps and clothes from the Salvation Army. Roger grew vegetables in the cramped back yard and visited his mother and father in their nearby high-rise. He rarely saw his two brothers — who also live in Latrobe — except at family gatherings.

He tended bar occasionally, but worried that the welfare people would find out and dock his welfare check. After a while, the effort of looking for work was too much, and he stopped.

In June 1987, I returned to Pennsylvania to interview Caldwell for a story on the 10th anniversary of the murders. He knew which day I would arrive, but not the time.

On my way to the airport car rental counter, someone called my name. I turned around, and saw a fat, white-haired man wearing a white shirt, cream-colored pants and red suspenders. It was Roger. I hadn't recognized him at first.

This time — 10 years after the murders and five years after his release from prison — Roger was morose and disheartened. Still no job, no money, no prospects. He was driving a 15-year-old station wagon his parents had lent him. But it had no brakes, as I found out when he asked me to drive.

For the first time, though, he began to talk about the murders. Until then, he'd refused to talk about the case, fearing that he'd be charged with perjury if he deviated from the sworn confession he'd given to Duluth officials in return for his freedom.

But now he was more open. There was a sense of doom in his words and in his manner. It was hard to tell if he didn't care any more about what happened or if he was talking to cleanse himself — to rid himself of some demons. Probably, it was some of each.

He said he hadn't committed the murders. He said he'd confessed only to get out of prison. "I was the patsy," he said. "An extremely wealthy person was murdered. Someone had to pay. My wife was the most hated person in the family, and the only way to get to her was through me."

He said he'd been home — in the Colorado hotel room — on the night of the murders. He sounded sincere, but he couldn't explain the evidence that had convicted him in Brainerd. He said he was framed, although he couldn't say by whom. Then he didn't want to talk about it any more.

It became clear that he was losing his will to live. As we drove together through the western Pennsylvania hills he pointed out old forts and historic buildings, and showed me Arnold Palmer's golf course and Mr. Rogers' boyhood home. During that drive, he made several foreboding remarks.

"I'm so disenchanted with the hand I've been dealt, but there's not a thing I can do about it."

"You reach a point in your life when you just give up. The older you get, the more bleak it becomes. When you're young, you haven't been kicked in the head enough to give up. But when you reach a certain age, you realize there's nothing out there. You're glad you've got a television and a little yard to putter in." (He was 53 at the time.)

"I'm sick. I'm probably dying. I'll be surprised if I'm here next year. I'll be downright amazed if I'm here next year."

Eleven months later — May 17, 1988 — Roger Caldwell killed himself. He cut his wrists with a steak knife in the kitchen of his little apartment. Relatives said he'd been drinking steadily for about two weeks.

Earlier in the week he'd told relatives that he was terminally ill, but a check with his doctor proved that was untrue.

In his apartment, police found a note: "What you need to know is that I didn't kill those girls, or, to my knowledge, ever harm a soul in my life."

It wasn't true, though. He'd beaten his girlfriend just days before the suicide, sending her to the hospital. Those close to the case believe that Caldwell was psychologically unable to admit, even to himself, that he'd killed the two women. He tried, to the end, to blot that memory from his mind.

On May 20, in the chapel of the Latrobe funeral home, eight relatives paid their last respects to Caldwell. The family allowed me to sit in on the service. It rained all day and into the night.

The Mayhem
Continues

In 1990, Marjorie and Wally Hagen moved into the tiny retirement community of Ajo, Arizona, pop. 3,500. She joined a church group, worked at the taco dinners and donated painted sweatshirts for a raffle.

They lived in a boxy house, four tiny rooms. Wally's health was poor — he was 82 now, and had cancer. Marjorie pushed him around town in a wheel chair, chatting with townspeople on the street.

Ajo, though, had a problem. A spate of arson fires plagued the town in late 1990 and early 1991. The burned homes were empty: either abandoned or owned by snowbirds from up north who escaped to Arizona each winter. Officials suspected a gang of youths was responsible for the fires, but couldn't catch anyone.

Then, on March 24, 1991, a neighbor of the Hagens saw someone approach his window and lay a cloth on the sill. He was very suspicious, because earlier that day someone had started a fire at a neighboring house by lighting a gasoline-soaked cloth on a windowsill.

So he called police, who staked out the area.

About 2 a.m., Hagen allegedly approached the neighbor's house and lit the rag. Police gave chase and caught her nearby. She was charged with two counts of arson and she was a suspect in 13 other suspicious fires.

Wally couldn't raise the $50,000 bond to free Marjorie from jail. "All I have is my Social Security," he said. "All the rest is tied up in judgments. And Marge's kids won't help - they say she's gotten into trouble too many times before. I think that's terrible, don't you?"

Wally said his wife was set up. He pointed to their dog, Wulf, and said: "There's the culprit. I think someone put meat juice on the rag and Wulf took it off the windowsill. She was just returning it."

He said he didn't know why someone would frame his wife.

"I'm standing by my wife," he said. "To my mind, she's innocent. I suppose you think it's strange I don't seem more upset. I suppose I should be, but things have always worked out in my life. I think this will, too."

The Hagens had earlier trouble in Arizona. They had property repossessed after a mobile home dealer accused them of writing a bad check for $55,000. And there was a second judgment for $450,000, said sheriff's officials.

The
Arson Trial

Marjorie stayed in jail for several months until Wally came up with the bail money. While Marjorie was "away," neighbors noticed a remarkable improvement in Wally's health. They said he didn't need his wheelchair anymore and was flirting with waitresses. And he started eating at his favorite restaurant, the local Kentucky Fried Chicken, where he wasn't allowed to eat when Marjorie was around.

Her lawyer successfully delayed the arson trial for 18 months, saying Wally was ill and needed his wife's attention.

When the trial finally began in Oct. 1992, Wally was called as one of the defense witnesses. In theatrical fashion, so typical of Marjorie, Wally was wheeled into the courtroom on a gurney while the entire courtroom watched in amazement. Then he gave his testimony lying down, with a "hearing ear dog" at his side.

Wally's story, this time, was that he and Marjorie had borrowed a towel from their neighbor and Marjorie was returning it when she put it on the window sill.

The jury was unimpressed by Wally's dramatic entrance and testimony. Court officials said the jurors had seen Wally getting out of a car, unaided, the day before, and were somewhat amused at the gurney ploy.

The jury found Marjorie Hagen guilty of attempted arson on Oct. 30, and because of her previous arson conviction, she faced a mandatory prison sentence.

Under Arizona law, she was supposed to go directly to jail to await final sentencing and any appeals. But Marjorie turned on her charm. She told the judge that Wally couldn't survive on his own and if she was going to prison she had to find someone to watch over him. She pleaded for just 24 hours of freedom, to take care of Wally.

The judge gave her one day more.

The New
Husband
Perishes

When Marjorie and Wally returned to Ajo, the local authorities were ready. Worried that Marjorie might make a break for Mexico, they kept an overnight watch on the house.

The next day, a sheriff's deputy smelled gas near the house. Tom Taylor, the lieutenant in the Pima County Sheriff's office who was overseeing the case, rushed over and knocked on the door. Marjorie came to a window and told Taylor that she'd accidently left the gas stove on earlier, but that it was off now and everything was okay.

She also said that she planned to live up to her promise to turn herself in later that afternoon.

Taylor went back to his office, but a couple hours later one of Marjorie's children telephoned from the Twin Cities saying Marjorie had just called to say Wally was dead.

Taylor and a team of officers hurried to the house and found Wally's body. Marjorie said she didn't know when he'd died. Police arrested her and charged her with murder.

"I hope they make this stick. I hope they put her away and throw away the key," said Jennifer Johnson, Marjorie's sister. The two women had not seen each other in years. Johnson said she was shocked, but not surprised at the latest turn of events.

Police found two suicide notes in the house, indicating that Wally may have believed he and Marjorie were entering into a suicide pact. But officials said they didn't think Marjorie ever had any intention of killing herself. A garden hose was found in the house, apparently used to funnel gas into the bedroom.

The suicide notes, though, complicated the case. Prosecutors knew it would be difficult to prove beyond a reasonable doubt that Marjorie had been involved in Wally's death.

Three weeks after Wally's death, Arizona officials announced they were temporarily dropping the murder charges.

They explained that under Arizona law, a grand jury must be convened or a preliminary hearing held soon after charges are filed. But many of the tests on Wally's body and other forensic evidence were not yet ready, so officials could not present their case in time to satisfy the law.

Because Marjorie was already in jail on the attempted arson case, there was no sense of urgency. But they said repeatedly that the charges would be refiled.

Autopsy results in the case proved quite interesting. Wally's body showed no signs of cancer, even though Marjorie had been claiming for years that he was dying of cancer. The couple made frequent forays into Mexico to buy medication that is unavailable in the U.S. She was frequently seen injecting substances into Wally.

Some of Wally's relatives said they had suspected for years that Marjorie was exaggerating his illness and using drugs to keep him passive.

And despite the apparent evidence that gas contributed to Wally's death, the official cause of death was determined to be an overdose of prescription pain killers. The prescription was in Wally's name.

In May 1993, Marjorie, still in prison, pleaded no contest to a charge that she set two fires at an Ajo repair shop, burning a car, a dump truck, a paint shed and two motor homes, including one owned by the Hagens worth about $35,000.

Finally, on June 12, 1993. Marjorie was sentenced to 15 years in prison for the two arson-related charges. Pima County Superior Court Judge Frank Dawley, the same judge who had released Marjorie after the conviction, gave her the maximum sentence allowable for the charges. He also ordered her to pay $39,000 in restitution to the damaged repair shop.

Under Arizona rules, she must serve at least 10 years before she is eligible for release, officials said. She was 59 at the time.

The same day, officials said they would not refile the murder charges, reasoning that Marjorie already had a hefty prison term ahead of her.

Taylor, the cop who'd pursued Marjorie on the arson cases and found Wally's body, had mixed feelings.

"I feel good that she got the maximum sentence on the arson charges, but I'm disappointed we couldn't make more progress on the murder charges," he said. "I would have liked to have had a jury look at all the facts."

Wally Hagen's family, too, was upset with the turn. They mourned the loss of their father and felt Marjorie was responsible. In a letter to Judge Dawley, two of the children wrote: "She's a career criminal and must be put away for the protection of society in general, and us specifically."

The Tour

Welcome to Glensheen.

Each year, the volunteer tour guides at Glensheen, the Congdon Mansion, show more than 100,000 people through the historic 39-room mansion on the shores of Lake Superior in Duluth.

During the official 75-minute tour, the guides point out the architectural highlights of the mansion -- the hand-carved woodwork, the gold leaf ceilings, the 15 bedrooms, the 15 fireplaces and eight bathrooms.

They also describe, in great detail, the outstanding furnishings found throughout the house:

"The light fixture in the reception room is carved alabaster. And the coffee table is made of in-laid marble."

"The silver lamps above the fireplace in the library came from Egypt."

The guides, however, do not tell you anything about the Congdon murders. So read the following pages closely before taking the tour. Then, when you tour the mansion, you'll know exactly what happened, and where.

If you've already taken the tour, and wondered about the murders, don't blame the tour guides. The University of Minnesota owns the mansion now, and university officials prefer not to discuss the murders. They've instructed the tour guides to say things like: "When Miss Congdon died . . ." or "Since the accident . . ."

One Glensheen guide said recently that someone in "nearly every tour group" asks about Miss Congdon's murder. Her answer, she said, is always the same. "We don't discuss it."

Ground Floor Plan

Caldwell's path → → → →

Rooms labeled in the plan: Milk Rm., Laundry, Lav., Coal, Wood, Storage, Boiler Room, Coal, Hall, Winter Garden, Cellar, Lav., Billard Room, Amusement Rm.

The Ground Floor

T he Glensheen Tour begins in the basement, referred to by the guides as the lower level, or the ground floor.

Although interesting, the first few minutes of the tour have no bearing on the murder case. Roger Caldwell was never in the laundry room or the milk room or the boiler room. Marjorie ran through that section of the house as a child, but, of course, the servants did all the work in those rooms.

Coming down the first long hallway on the tour, take note of the stairway on the left, and then pay great attention to the billiard room. Caldwell broke a window in the rear alcove of that room. He made his way around the ancient billiard table and into the hallway, then up the stairs toward Miss Congdon's bedroom.

Through the rear windows in the billiard room, and in the amusement room next door, you can see the patio area, or the subway, as the Congdon family called it.

On the night of the murders, the exterior windows had been removed from this area, so Caldwell was able to walk right in and easily break into the billiard room. Caldwell says he doesn't remember what he used to break the window. Police believe it was probably a rock or a tool that he found nearby.

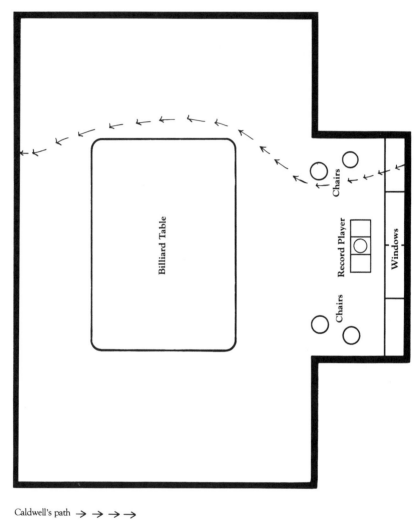

Caldwell's path → → → →

Billiard Room

The
Billiard
Room

Roger Caldwell entered the mansion by breaking one of the windows in the billiard room —— one of the middle windows in the room's rear alcove. He smashed a small hole in the window with a heavy object, scattering glass more than 16 feet across the room. He reached into the hole and unlatched the window lock, opened the window and climbed into the room.

During Roger Caldwell's trial, there was a great deal of discussion about the size of the hole in the window, and the size of Caldwell's biceps, and whether he could have reached into the hole and opened the latch.

Police investigators found a 6-by-4 inch hole in the double locked window. During the investigation, five Duluth policemen tried to reach through the hole to undo the locks and open the window. Only one officer, Barry Brooks, was successful.

Police measured Caldwell's arms, and found his biceps and forearms were less than half-an-inch larger than Brooks's. Police were satisfied that Caldwell's arms would have fit.

But defense attorney Doug Thomson was not satisfied. He created a cardboard replica of the window, with the middle cut out to represent the hole, complete with cardboard shards of glass. During Roger's trial, he asked Brooks to reach through the hole.

Halfway through, Brooks's arm caught on a cardboard shard. He wiggled his arm the rest of the way through the hole. "So your arm doesn't fit?" Thomson asked. "Well, I made it through," Brooks replied.

In his confession, Caldwell said simply that he "reached all the way through" the window and unlocked it.

"I remember walking past a pool table and getting to the stairs and my intention was to get up to Miss Congdon's bedroom," he said.

The billiard table, incidentally, has been in that room since 1909, according to the guides.

First Floor Plan

The
First
Floor

As the tour moves up the stairs, from the ground floor to the first floor, you will follow in Roger Caldwell's footsteps.

He carried no flashlight that night. Feeling his way along the wall in the dark, he reached the main floor, then continued up the stairs.

The official tour, however, branches off to examine the rest of the main floor before continuing upstairs.

The library, with its large marble fireplace and Angora goat's wool wallcovering, is where Roger Caldwell met with Miss Elisabeth on his visit to the mansion one month before the murders.

The two, mother-in-law and her new son-in-law, chatted for about half an hour in the library. He brought her a tiny Chinese carved horse, a gift from Marjorie, and told her about Colorado. Roger had come to Duluth, without his wife, to ask the trustees of the Congdon estate for money. But he did not discuss money with Miss Congdon.

In a meeting that day with the trustees, Roger's request was turned down.

Except for the front door and hallway, Roger never saw the rest of the mansion's main floor. The night of the murders, Roger raced down the stairway after killing the two women, but he was quite drunk, and probably didn't even notice the ornamental glass, or the floor-to-ceiling oak paneling, or the Oriental rugs in the hallway.

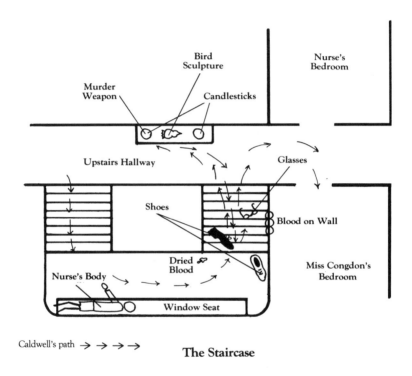

Bird
Sculpture

Murder
Weapon

Candlesticks

Nurse's
Bedroom

Upstairs Hallway

Glasses

Shoes

Blood on Wall

Dried
Blood

Miss Congdon's
Bedroom

Nurse's Body

Window Seat

Caldwell's path → → → →

The Staircase

The Staircase

As Roger Caldwell inched his way up the stairway that night, between the main floor and the second floor, he suddenly heard a door open at the top of the stairs, and the night nurse, Velma Pietila, appeared above him with a flashlight.

They struggled for a moment at the top of the stairs, then she fell to the mid-level landing below. Roger took a brass candlestick holder — the left one, from a set of two on a table beside him — and went down to the nurse. He hit her repeatedly.

They struggled again. She clawed at his head, pulling out pieces of hair. Blood spattered on the wall, halfway between the top and the landing. Pools of blood collected on the landing.

Pietila's flashlight, now broken, lay near the top of the steps. Her shoes were off, one partway up the stairs, the other on the landing. Her glasses were also found on the stairs.

When the relief nurse arrived at 7 the next morning, she found Pietila's body on the landing, lying on the window seat overlooking the mansion grounds and Lake Superior.

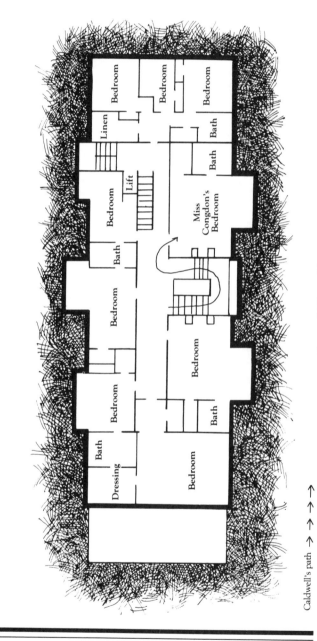

Second Floor Plan

Caldwell's path → → → →

The Second Floor

T he tour continues on the second floor, through the impressive array of bedrooms with their fireplaces and unique furnishings.

Don't ask which bedroom was Elisabeth Congdon's. The guides won't tell you.

When you walk up the main stairs to the second floor, it's the first bedroom around to the right, looking out on the lake.

For a time after the murders, Miss Congdon's bedroom was used as a meeting room, lined with dozens of chairs. In 1983, though, it once again became a bedroom.

Just across the hall from Miss Congdon's room, is a small bathroom where the killer washed up after the murders. Blood was spattered in the bathroom, and police found a mysterious fingerprint on the sink. It was definitely not Caldwell's print, police said. For a while, the print was known as the "mystery print."

Further investigation, however, showed that the print belonged to Police Sgt. Gary Waller, chief investigator in the case.

There are servant's quarters on the second floor of the mansion, separated from the main bedrooms by a heavy door. A cook was sleeping there on the night of the murders. She was awakened about 2:45 early that morning, when her black poodle, "Muffin" began barking.

The cook took the dog with her as she went to the bathroom. On the way back to her room, the dog leaped from her arms and ran to the heavy door separating the two sections. The cook brought the dog back to her room, but Muffin kept whining until 5 a.m.

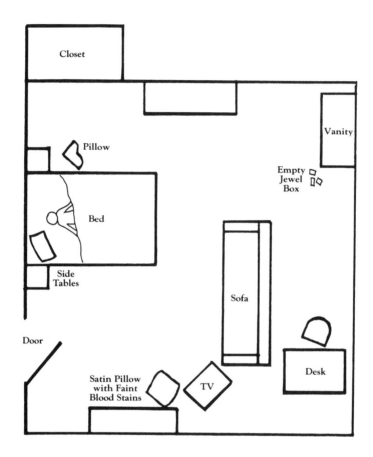

Closet

Pillow

Vanity

Empty
Jewel
Box

Bed

Side
Tables

Sofa

Door

Satin Pillow
with Faint
Blood Stains

TV

Desk

Miss Congdon's Bedroom

The Victim's Bedroom

Elisabeth Congdon went to sleep about 10:50 p.m. on Sunday night, June 26, 1977. She had just returned from a weekend outing on the Brule River in Wisconsin. She was tired, but very happy, according to an attendant.

Her bed, that night, was just to the left of the door. A davenport, desk, television, chest of drawers and vanity filled the rest of the room.

The killer entered the room, long after she'd fallen asleep. He pulled a satin pillow from beneath her head, and held it over her face. She tried to escape, but couldn't.

The killer then searched through her vanity and chest of drawers. He found a small wicker basket in the closet, and filled it with jewelry. He took a watch and ring from Miss Congdon's hand and put them in the basket.

Then he took a gold, Byzantine coin from a memorabilia box on the desk.

He left the room to wash up in the bathroom across the hall. He found the nurse's car keys in the adjoining bedroom, then hurried down the stairs and out the front door. There, he found the nurse's car and drove it to the Minneapolis/St. Paul International Airport.

The next morning, police found a satin pillow, with faint blood stains, on the floor near the fireplace. Empty jewelry boxes were scattered by the vanity, in the corner diagonally opposite the doorway.

Miss Congdon, 83-years-old and partially paralyzed, was lying in her bed, dead.

The Confession

These are edited excerpts of Roger Caldwell's confession to the murders of Elisabeth Congdon and Velma Pietila. The confession was made July 5, 1983, at the St. Louis County Courthouse in Duluth.

Prosecutor John DeSanto asked the questions. Roger Caldwell answered.

Q Do you understand that if you say something here that is not truthful, you could subject yourself to perjury charges for any untruthful statements made in answer to the questions here this afternoon in the library, do you understand that?

A I do.

Q Also, Mr. Caldwell, do you understand that it is agreed as part of this plea negotiation agreement that you would receive no further incarceration for the new convictions of murder in the second degree, that you would be sentenced simply to time served or if there was an 111 month sentence, any further sentence would be simply suspended. Do you understand that? You would receive no further time in jail?

A I do.

Q Now with regard to the murders of Elisabeth Congdon and Velma Pietila, would you state, in your own words, when the incident which led to those murders was first planned or discussed with anyone?

A There was no plan of murder.

Q All right. With regard to the murders that occurred, these murders that occurred on June 27th of 1977, would you, in your own words, simply state how it came about that you committed those murders?

A The intent was burglary. I was surprised in the act of the commission of the burglary by the nurse who was totally unknown to me. She was loud and aggressive. I tried to silence her.

Q Mr. Caldwell, do you know that that's kind of hard to believe that you don't remember the name used to buy the airplane ticket?

A Well, yes, I can understand how it's hard to believe, but as you well know with the investigation you conducted, I am an old drunk. I have been on the sauce for a long, long time. I have been treated for alcoholism on two different occasions and have wandered in and out of Alcoholics Anonymous heaven knows how many times over the years, and in time of stress, I mean I would maintain a glow all day, everyday, seven days a week, year after year. Not just periodically, this was a constant, ongoing thing. I am not using – trying to imply that drunkenness was a defense, that's out of the question because drunkenness was my normal state and sometimes worse.

Q That's what you are attributing your failure to remember the name that you used to travel?

A There were many things that I don't remember throughout my life that were nearer and dearer to me than a false name I would give at an airline counter. I don't recall the names of uncles and aunts and nieces and nephews.

Q Okay.

A No. As our situation progressed, as it became apparent after our marriage that Marjorie was – well, she was simply a terrible liar, that's all she did to me constantly. Not at first, but then the longer we were married the worse it got and it became – I tried to defend her. I believed her. I loved her.

Q Now, you fly then to Minneapolis. What time do you get to Minneapolis?

A It was daylight.

Q Daylight. What do you do when you get to Minneapolis?

A Well, tried to figure out where Duluth was. I didn't know. I had only been here once before in my life.

Q Okay. What did you do now once you got to Minneapolis Airport when you have come, as you say, to burglarize the mansion?

A Well, tried to figure a way to get from there to Duluth and I must have flown up (on the one previous visit) but I wasn't all that impressed with your Duluth Airport and it dawned on me that the police would certainly be checking transportation and one of the shuttle flights from the Twin Cities up to here would be probably too easy to trace and pinpoint me, so I toyed with the idea of taking a cab but then I thought, too, I honestly didn't have any knowledge of the distance.

Q So what did you eventually do?

A I wandered around and asked people directions and wound up taking a bus.

Q A bus from where?

A From the bus station in the Twin Cities on up here to Duluth.

Q And what name did you use to get your bus ticket?

A I don't know that there is a name required.

Q And do you recall when you got to Duluth, what time of day it was?

A Late afternoon or early evening, I suppose.

Q Then what did you do?

A Well, I had a few more drinks.

Q Where did you have the drinks?...In a bar in Duluth?

A Oh, yes, Oh yeah.

Q Then what did you do?

A I waited until dark. And in discussions at the bar found out how the cab service worked in town and took a taxi cab out to London Road. I didn't even know the address...I told him I would tell him where to let me out. I didn't know for certain where I was going but I would recognize the site when I saw it.

Q Where did you get out?

A Well, I recognized the mansions, other big homes sitting off to the right, and when I got to where I thought the Congdon home was, I had him then let me out a few blocks up London Road.

Q Do you recall during the early part of the investigation, after your arrest, when we had a cab driver look at you in a lineup?

A I do.

Q Was that the cab driver?

A I have no idea.

Q Were you frightened he might identify you?

A Yes I was. But I don't have any idea if that's who it was. It may very well have been. I don't know.

Q You went from the bus to a bar and then you took a cab out to the mansion when it got dark?

A Your bus terminal, as I recall, seemed to be in a rather seedy place, in a rather seedy neighborhood, which was fine for my purposes and there were several bars in the area and I just chose one of them, a real working-man's bar.

Q Okay. You get (out of the cab.) Then what did you do?

A It was just approaching darkness and in my mind I thought it best to wait until the house was still and people were sleeping and I had only ever been there one other time and had never poked around or seen the grounds, so I was totally unfamiliar with the geography and I didn't want to linger on the street, on London Road. I didn't know whether it was a prominent thoroughfare. As I say, I am not acquainted with Duluth.

Q Where did you wait?

A First, I walked back past the house so I would make sure I knew where I was and walked clear past it and there was a little cemetery on the same side of the street as the house that wasn't in good maintenance and looked like it didn't get a lot of traffic and I waited in there. (When it got dark enough) I left there and went over to the house.

Q Are you drinking on the hooch?

A Yeah. I was seldom without one.

Q What kind of booze was it, do you know?

A Vodka. A pint.

Q Where did you get in (to the mansion)?

A Through the window.

Q What did you use to break the window?

A Something on the porch, or there was an odd, it's not a room, you couldn't even call it a sun porch that this window faced out on, that was filled with clutter and I would imagine I found an object there to break the window with.

Q What did you do after you got into the mansion through the window?

A I remember walking past a pool table and getting to the stairs and my intention was to get up to Miss Congdon's bedroom, where I assumed, whatever valuables of small size that can be easily carried would be found.

Q Did you know where the bedroom would be located?

A No I didn't.

Q Had Marjorie talked with you about that?

A Marjorie and I never — The only talking we did about the mansion was the time she had spent there as a child and in growing-up years, but we never discussed specifics about the physical arrangements of the house other than to tell me about the boat house and the groundskeeper's house and the old greenhouses. We never went into any details about the floor plan of the house or the arrangements.

Q Then what happens?

A Then I started up the stairs. I wasn't expecting a confrontation...The house was dark, it was late at night. I assumed people were sleeping and I meant no harm.

Q Had you discussed that in any way with Marjorie Caldwell? Whether someone would be there or not?

A No.

Q Did you know about Elisabeth Congdon having around-the-clock nurses?

A Yes, I did know that.

Q Now, you get to the staircase, what happened?

A Well, I started up the stairs and immediately roused the nurse, which surprised me as much as it did her, I'm sure. I guess I was on the landing (between the first and second floors) and she was either still coming down the stairs or had reached the landing.

Q What happens there?

A Well, she shouted and struck out at me. I don't know that she had anything in her hand or not. She may have had.

Q What did you do?

A Struck back. (There was) a fight.

Q Is the nurse killed at that time?

A No, no. I suppose she was unconscious because then I went up to the second floor and, as I recall, she had let out a moan or something to indicate that she was still, if not awake or alert, still making noises...I found the candlestick and went back down and beat her with it to quiet her down.

Q What did you do then after beating the nurse to death?

A Well, I didn't beat her to death. I beat her and she died.

Q What did you do after that?

A Well, that quieted her and there was a light on in a room. I poked in there, looked in and saw Miss Congdon was in there and I didn't wish to — she was obviously sleeping and I knew she was not a well woman, I didn't want to disturb her...so I thought, better if I can obstruct her hearing. Anyway, I took the pillow and put it over her head, more to block out light and sound than anything else.

Q You know that the physical evidence in the investigation showed a blood type that (was) consistent with your blood on the bedspread and the pillow under Elisabeth Congdon's head. Would that have been because you were cut in the struggle with the nurse?

A The nurse bit my finger.

Q Do you recall turning the shoe of the nurse on her which resulted in those little puncture wounds on her head and arms?

A I don't recall any detail of that. I was so terrified and panicked by what I was obviously caught up in, that it was just – it all happened so quickly.

Q So you are admitting the murder of Elisabeth Congdon, is that true?

A Well, I guess I am admitting to the murder of her, except murder wasn't the intention.

Q What did you do after you put the pillow over her face? What did you do in her room?

A I wanted to get out as quick as I could. I was obviously in a heck of a mess and wanted to get out of there and out of Duluth and out of Minnesota just as quickly as I could, so I ransacked drawers to look for valuables, took what I could find and left.

Q Do you remember taking the ring off Elisabeth Congdon's finger...(or) taking the watch off her wrist?

A I have no recollection of it...I was in such a state of terror I couldn't move quick enough to get out.

Q Do you remember taking the wicker basket?

A I don't remember taking it.

Q The drawers on Elisabeth Condgon's dresser were all pulled out evenly. Why were the drawers so even?

A I don't know anything about burglary. I have never stolen anything in my life. I certainly never burglarized anybody. I have never caused any damage to anyone that I can recall in a lifetime, other than what I may have done when I was drunk. I have never burglarized a home.

Q Why did you take jewelry items?

A Well, it seemed to be a logical thing of small size and great value.

Q What were you going to do with the jewelry items?

A I hadn't thought that far ahead...the purpose was to sell and convert to cash.

Q Did you have any conversation with the nurse, Velma Pietila, before your confrontation with her?

A No, I didn't.

Q Did you take the coin from the mansion?

A That's another mystery. I don't have any recollection of that coin at all.

Q (Then) where did you go, what did you do?

A There was another room across the hall which also had a light on and I was looking for a bathroom. I had blood on me. Surprisingly little, but, nonetheless, blood.

Q The washroom where you washed up was near at hand to the room where you found the keys. Where did you find the keys?

A They were laying on the bed...They were obviously car keys. I think I even peeked out the window and saw the car in the front of the house and I went back on downstairs and out.

Q You passed Velma Pietila's body there?

A I did.

Q Then you get out the front door, what do you do?

A Went immediately to the car, match the keys and took off for the Twin Cities.

Q Did you, by chance, during the time you were in the mansion, hear the dog barking?

A I did not. I heard nothing. The only sound I heard was the sounds given off by the nurse.

Q In going to the mansion, as you say to simply burglarize it, to steal from it, what was your original intention of how you were going to get away with this?

A I had no plan. I was drunker than a lord, without any — I had no plan. I had nothing. I was stupid. I was — I had no prior experience along those lines. I have never in my life broken into anything.

Q If you're going to commit burglary, though, didn't you have some plan as far as how you were going to get away with the goods?

A No, I didn't.

Q It was just lucky that the keys for the car happened to be there.

A Just dumb luck that the keys for the car happened to be there.

Q What do you remember about the trip (from Duluth to Minneapolis)?

A I remember that I had a bottle with me and I was sipping at that, too.

Q A bottle of what? How much, what kind was it, where had you gotten the bottle?

A I don't know if I brought it with me on the plane or bought it here in Duluth. It was a pint bottle. It fit in the hip pocket.

Q You entered the mansion, then, with the bottle in your pocket?

A Oh sure. I wouldn't be without it.

Q How did you get back from Minneapolis to Colorado?

A Flew.

Q Commercial airlines?

A Oh, yes. Well, again, I don't have any idea which one. It was a commercial flight.

Q What about purchasing the suede bag?

A It's hard to believe that. That is, I don't recall that.

Q How did you feel when you saw we were unable to put you on an airline?

A Dumb lucky. I know I recall our trial, the three months that you and I spent in court, vividly. I was quite sober at the time and I know through the evidence that you presented the lengths you went to put me on an airline and the hours that were spent in trying to get me there and I couldn't imagine how you missed me.

Q (Back in Colorado) why did you make the phone call to Marj?

A Well, I had no transportation. I don't know whether you ever uncovered this in your investigation, but it wasn't particularly uncommon for me to go off and disappear. I mean this certainly wasn't the first time that happened. At least on several occasions when Marj and I would get into horrendous arguments — her temper was far worse than mine ever will be and she would simply infuriate me and I am not, pardon me for saying so, I am not a violent man and I didn't fight with her or anybody else. I would get very upset with her and my escape has always been booze and on several occasions during our marriage I would just simply get in the car and drive off and go somewhere and get bombed and be gone sometimes, many times, overnight, sometimes two, maybe three nights.

Q What did you do with the jewelry after you are back in Colorado? How does the jewelry get in the blue container with Marj's?

A I put it there.

Q When did you do that?

A That night, I think. I know this is difficult for you and it's difficult for me, but you don't —maybe you do know, I don't know what you know, John, but I was on the sauce awful heavy.

Q Mr. Caldwell, when you go open that safety deposit box (and put the June 24th assignment of inheritance in it) you know Elisabeth Congdon is dead, you have murdered her, right?

A Right. I didn't know I had murdered her, no. I knew she was dead. I never thought it was murder.

Q You are not denying doing what caused her death?

A I am not denying that, no.

Q With regard to Elisabeth Congdon, though, then as a result of your actions, the physical evidence somewhat contradicts what you are telling us. I mean, obviously there was more done than simply placing a pillow over her head so that she wouldn't hear, so that you could shut out the light and any noise and if it doesn't jive with the physical evidence, it leads us to question, was there somebody else in the house with you that actually killed her?

A There was nobody else in that house with me. I don't recall doing any more (to her).

Q The physical evidence shows us that she had — that a pillow was placed firmly enough over her that she struggled underneath it so that skin was scraped from her nose and you're aware of that physical evidence?

A Yes, I am.

Q Based on that, do you have any dispute that there must have been some struggle by her underneath that pillow as you held it over her?

A I don't recall the struggle.

Q What reaction did Marjorie have, when she picked you up at the restaurant (in Colorado)?

A Anxious, hurried. She had been real-estating again. She had seen some properties and was telling me about them and wanting to hurry back up to the animals.

Q What did you say to her about where you had been?

A Virtually nothing. She never had a great deal of interest. I told her something to the effect (that I had) a session with the lawyer and I had been off tooting and she didn't want to hear about it. She didn't like listening to stories of drunks.

Q You understand that if she is involved, whether it be before the fact or after the fact, at this stage she is not going to face any criminal consequences. She has the benefit of what we call the double jeopardy clause. Do you understand that?

A Yes, of course I do. Yes.

Q I don't want you to sit here with some kind of motive to cover up for her, to protect her. She virtually is home free, do you understand what I am saying?

A Yes, John. I have more reason to implicate her than I have not to implicate her.

Q Don't you think you're getting the short end of the stick right now?

A I know I am getting the short end of the stick, but not financially. I never had any claim to it. I didn't marry Marj for her money. When I married her, I didn't even know she had money. I had never heard of the Congdons.

Q Why is it then, if you say Marjorie knew nothing about your going to Duluth, why does she alibi for you?

A Trying to find reasons for what Marjorie ever has done is something that none of us are able to do, including me.

Q Wouldn't you admit that that would point to some knowledge on her part, it's somewhat reasonable to assume she knows where you have gone...?

A No...She would come up with an awful lot of spur of the moment explanations for anything and everything to total strangers...All that I can guess is Marj knew I was off on a toot. That was a source of embarrassment to her. She didn't like to be embarrassed and she would, rather than just stay quiet, she would feel compelled to – she's a compulsive talker – she would feel compelled to explain away my absence.

Q Hadn't you planned any alibi statements on her part for you?

A No.

Q What about when you came to Duluth for the funeral? Do you do anything with Marjorie as far as covering up your activities and involvement in the murder? Do you do anything, talk with her about it?

A She had no knowledge of it and, as best I knew, nobody did at that point.

Q You told no one?

A No, I had no reason to.

Q Have you been offered any money to protect her?

A None whatever.

Q Has Marjorie ever called you and asked you about this?

A I haven't seen or spoken with Marjorie since approximately three weeks after her acquittal. She came to visit me in prison. She was rather cool toward me and, as it turned out, at the time I wasn't aware of it, but as it turned out the only reason for the visit was to ask me if I wanted to continue having Doug (Thomson) representing me, or if I wanted Ron Meshbesher to visit me. I said no, I think I will stick with Doug. And as I noodled over the years I realize that that was goodbye for us and I have never laid eyes on her or spoken with her since.

Q Did Marjorie ever ask you after you were charged whether you did it?

A No. That never came up. At the time I was arrested and charged and for the months that I spent in jail in Duluth, she visited me, she brought me items. We talked as best we could under the circumstances, through the bars and what have you. She seemed to be standing by me and supporting me in every way she could. There was never any question that I was guilty. There was never any – never any from her.

Q Did she ask you about where you were when it looked like what happened here was consistent with you committing the murders?

A No. She never connected one with the other. As I say, it had long since stopped being a surprise — when we would get into a real argument that I would go off and go out on a toot. So this was far from the first time that had happened. I had left her high and dry before.

Q Who do you think is getting left high and dry now?

A Me.

The Chronology

June 27, 1977: Elisabeth Congdon, wealthy Duluth heiress, is found murdered in her bed, smothered with a pillow. Her night nurse, Velma Pietila, was bludgeoned to death on the stairway of the 39-room Congdon mansion. Officially, police say robbery was the motive. But privately, they have already begun investigating Roger and Marjorie Caldwell, Congdon's daughter and son-in-law.

July 6, 1977: Police arrest Roger Caldwell and eventually charge him with committing the murders, allegedly to speed the collection of his wife's hefty share of the inheritance.

July 15, 1977: University of Minnesota officials, who own the Congdon Mansion under the terms of Elisabeth Congdon's will, discuss what to do with the property. Some suggestions: A Scandinavian Resource Center, a retreat for the arts, or a center for the study of Lake Superior. Eventually, officials decide to offer tours of the mansion. The tours prove to be successful.

September 6, 1977: Four of Marjorie Caldwell's seven children from a previous marriage ask a court to disqualify their mother from sharing in the inheritance, if she is found to be involved in the murders.

April 10, 1978: Roger Caldwell's trial begins in Brainerd, Minn., moved from Duluth because of extensive publicity about the case. It takes nearly a month to pick a jury, and then nearly two months for testimony in the case.

July 8, 1978: The jury finds Caldwell guilty of both murders. Deliberations take three days.

July 10, 1978: Caldwell is sentenced to two consecutive life terms in prison.

July 11, 1978: Encouraged by Roger Caldwell's conviction, Duluth officials charge Marjorie Caldwell with conspiring to kill her mother and the nurse. She is released on $100,000 bond.

April 2, 1979: Marjorie Caldwell's trial begins in Hastings, again moved because of pre-trial publicity.

July 21, 1979: The jury deliberates nine hours and finds Marjorie Caldwell not guilty of the charges. After the trial, jurors throw a party and invite Marjorie.

July 25, 1979: Roger Caldwell's attorneys ask for a new trial, based on the evidence from his wife's trial.

August 7, 1981: Marjorie Caldwell and Wallace Hagen of Mound, Minn., are wed in Valley City, N.D. Roger Caldwell apparently didn't learn of the wedding until two years later. He claims that he and Marjorie were not divorced.

August 6, 1982: The Minnesota Supreme Court grants Roger Caldwell a new trial, citing the new evidence from Marjorie's trial. Roger Caldwell is released from prison, after serving more than five years, and goes home to Latrobe, Pennsylvania, to await a new trial.

March 1983: North Dakota officials file bigamy charges against Marjorie Caldwell. She will not be extradited, they say, so she faces prosecution only if she returns to North Dakota.

May 31, 1983: Marjorie Caldwell and her children reach an out-of-court settlement in the inheritance dispute. She gets one-fourth of a family trust set up by her mother and she will draw the income from one-third of her children's share until she dies. A good chunk of the inheritance, perhaps as much as $2 million, goes for attorney's fees.

July 5, 1983: Roger Caldwell and Duluth officials agree to a plea bargain in the murder case: Roger pleads guilty to second degree murder, and in return, he does not have to serve any more time in prison.

January 13, 1984: Marjorie Caldwell Hagen is convicted of arson and insurance fraud in connection with a 1982 fire at a house in Mound. She is sentenced to 2$^1/_2$ years in prison.

January 26, 1985: Her appeal is turned down, and Marjorie Caldwell begins serving her prison term for the arson and fraud conviction.

October 22, 1986: Marjorie Caldwell is released from prison, after serving about 21 months.

May 17, 1988: Roger Caldwell kills himself in a small Latrobe apartment where he lived with a girlfriend. Only nine people attend his funeral service three days later.

March 24, 1991: Marjorie is arrested in Ajo, Arizona, and charged with trying to burn down two houses. Police suspect her in 13 other suspicious fires in the small retirement community.

October 29, 1992: Marjorie is convicted of attempted arson. Although she is supposed to go immediately to jail, she convinces the judge to give her 24 hours of freedom "to take care of Wally."

October 30, 1992: Wally Hagen is found dead in his home, apparently gassed to death. Later, officials say he died of a drug overdose. Marjorie is charged with murder, but the charges are later dropped. She's sentenced to 15 years in prison on the attempted arson conviction and must serve at least 10 years.

The
Author

Joe Kimball, a reporter for the Minneapolis Star Tribune, happened to be in Duluth on the day of the Congdon murders. He wrote about the murder investigation and the two trials, and interviewed Roger Caldwell in Pennsylvania following Caldwell's release from prison.

Additional copies of this book are available by mail for $5.95 plus $1.00 for postage and handling.

Send payment to: Jaykay Publishing, Inc.
P.O. Box 15775
Mpls., MN 55415

This publication was produced, illustrated, and designed by Albarella & Associates, Inc., St. Paul, Minnesota